HUNGER OF THE HEART
Communion at the Wall

LARRY POWELL

ACKNOWLEDGEMENTS

I offer my most sincere thanks to my children, Neil and Tish, and to my wife, Betty, for granting me the space and the time to heal and for giving me their unconditional love and support.

My thanks go also to Dave LaBelle, my mentor and friend, for convincing me that I had something important to say through photography. I am grateful to Mike Morse and Jack Corn for their inspiration and friendship that helped me see in new directions. I send my deepest thanks to Dr. Charles Bussey for his enthusiasm and unending support. And to Kim Hughes, I extend warm regards for her insight and sheer stamina.

Note: The photos in this publication are used for illustrative purposes only. No relationship necessarily exists between the persons in the photos and the writings. You will also note that the quotes have been shown just as they were left at the Wall. The spelling and grammar have not been changed.

Credits:
Text: Cara Sutherland, Curator of the Museum of Our National Heritage
Conception: Bob Smith, Carlisle Publishing Services, Dubuque, Iowa
Author Photo: Dave LaBelle

Book Team
Publisher: Sandra J. Hirstein
Managing Editor: Mary Jo Graham
Assistant Editor: Sharon K. Cruse
Designer: Bob Neumann

Copyright (c) 1995 by Larry Powell.

All rights reserved.

Published by Islewest Publishing,
a division of Carlisle Communications,
4242 Chavenelle Drive,
Dubuque, IA 52002.
1-800-557-9867

Manufactured in the United States of America.

ISBN 0-9641919-4-6

DEDICATION

This work is dedicated to the volunteers at the
Vietnam Veterans Memorial,
who not only give of their time,
but also of their hearts.

In appreciation for their generosity and dedication, a percentage of the proceeds from
this publication are being donated to Friends of the Vietnam Veterans Memorial.

I feel the unutterable longing,
Thy hunger of the heart is mine;
I reach and grope for hands in darkness,
My ear grows sharp for voice or sign.

John Greenleaf Whittier, "To Lydia Maria Child," 1870. *Complete Writings*, 7 vols., 1904.

FOREWARD

Still haunted by yesterday and last night, we are drawn to the Vietnam Veterans Memorial—"The Wall." Under the dark cover of the early dawn we come, before the tourists and the crowds arrive. We hope and pray that at this hallowed place we might somehow be able to commune with loved ones whose bodies have been taken from us, and whose eternal souls live in a place we cannot see or touch. But mostly we come to be healed, and to seek an end to the nightmares that refuse to set us free. We leave forever changed.

At this healing wall, before 56,196 silent witnesses, we leave our gifts: Glass. Paper. Medal. Wood. Cloth. Ashes. Prayers. Tears. Love.

Each gift is a meaningful, personal tribute, a thread between the living and the dead, tying the present to the past.

A veteran of the Vietnam War, Larry Powell, like many of those he photographs, is drawn to the memorial again and again to witness and to share. Driven by a belief that the world should not forget that Vietnam is not over for thousands of suffering survivors, he has worked nearly a decade documenting those who visit the Wall. His photographs are poignant testaments of love and painful reminders of war's ugly legacy.

Through his documentary images, we are invited to share, to study our neighbor's pain, and to visually sort through their personal treasures and expressions of love. We are allowed to handle another's precious belongings with the fingers of our eyes and hearts, to pour over our survivors' intimate grief. We visually caress the fur of a stuffed animal that brought comfort and protection to a little boy on frightening nights, or take into our hearts the private words of love and fear sent to loved ones in far away places. We can look deep into trusting, hope-filled eyes, proudly speaking to us from endless pages of high school yearbooks.

The beauty and strength of Powell's photographs lie in their straightforwardness, their plainness. His images are not loud or glitzy. They are not contrived compositions dressed in flashy colors or studio light. His photographs do not shout or call attention to themselves, or steal the voice of their subjects. Instead,

Powell's images are honest paths that lead us gently to places we know we should go.

Furthermore, by documenting instead of staging, as so many photographers feel a need to do, Powell allows us to see and experience both people and emblems more purely, without the clutter of another's vision or interpretation. His photographs have an honesty and integrity that grows harder to find in the photojournalism community. As we view these images, we are subtly reminded of the power of the still, documentary photograph to warn, educate, and involve us. Larry Powell's photographic sketches help us see others and ourselves more clearly and more compassionately.

Powell's images are valuable and rich because he preserves the environment in which they were recorded. To have the opportunity to study those who come to the Wall and examine the personal gifts they leave at its base, as they appeared, is no small thing. Environment provides us context. The Wall, the people, the gifts are one. Remove the expressions of love from the sacred Wall where they were placed, or change the position in which they were offered, and each scene loses its virtue.

Viewed through photographic eyes, Powell's photographs are to be admired and scrutinized for their aesthetic value, for the richness of their tones, and their artistic composition. Yet if we are to see truly the beauty and the worth of these images, we cannot afford to be blinded by the craft. Let us look with our hearts and our imaginations, beyond the expressions and compositions, beyond the gifts of paper and cloth and glass, and see the weeping hearts that ache to be comforted and are not. More importantly, let us see the eternal love that cannot be killed.

With his caring and photographic skills, Powell continues to build healing bridges between anguish and acceptance. Because of his efforts, many individuals have been freed from dark cells of grief and denial, and have been led to the light that shines from sharing and forgiving.

Like those he photographs, he too leaves gifts. His offerings are not flowers or medals, but images, photographs of people like you and me trying to cope. His photographs remind us that for thousands of suffering souls their war is not over.

When I met Larry Powell in 1987, his photographic skills were elementary, but his enthusiasm for photojournalism was unparalleled. He was hungry to know and grow, and he poured himself into his work the way he attacks everything he sets his mind to do. I encouraged him to use photojournalism as a tool to learn about himself and as a voice to communicate his feelings. I had no idea then how far his skills would take him. He has blossomed into a gifted story-teller, and he has made many meaningful contributions with his photography.

Dave LaBelle
Photojournalist-In-Residence
Western Kentucky University

PREFACE

Following military withdrawal from Vietnam in 1973 and the closing of the Embassy in 1975, Americans wanted to forget the years of conflict—both abroad and at home. Yet America could not let go. The unanswered questions of the POWs and MIAs reminded us that the war was not over in the hearts of many. There was a need to confront the reality of war, the consequences of which were shaping future generations. Although we wanted to forget, each year brought new memories to the surface. Vietnam was part of our culture. America needed to deal with this memory in order to move into the future. Commonly known as the "Wall," the Vietnam Veterans Memorial marks a nation's coming to terms with its history.

I was born in 1959, the year that the first casualties' names appear on the Wall. While I was attending school during the sixties and seventies, I was aware that the war was going on, but it never really touched my life. Or so I thought.

In 1993, my job brought me to the Capitol to work on an exhibition focusing on the Vietnam Veterans Memorial Collection. Since the dedication of the memorial in 1982, people have been leaving notes or mementoes in honor of someone whose name is on the Wall. These mementoes convey lasting emotional impact of the Vietnam War on Americans. Since the early 1980s, the National Park Service[1] has collected and cared for the relics and memorabilia left by visitors at the Wall. These objects are unique to the place and the history of the memorial and now compose an important museum collection, which numbers over 30,000 items. These materials are preserved by the National Park Service for future generations to learn from the Vietnam experience.

As a curator, I was to spend the next year culling through the collection, choosing articles for an exhibition that was scheduled to open in late 1994 at the Museum of Our National Heritage. In order to know what would be appropriate and meaningful to the people who would visit this exhibit, I needed to understand the context that surrounded these artifacts—to see the articles as they were left at the Wall and to watch the people who brought them. I needed to be at the Wall where the story of this collection began.

The exhibition required a sense of place. Photography would meet that need. I worked with several photographers who documented the Wall and its related statues. We spent every day at the Wall, arriving at dawn and leaving after dark. While the photographers captured images, I talked to people. More importantly I listened. I listened to veterans, to their wives and children, to their parents, and to foreign journalists sent to cover the dedication of the new Women's Statue. All shared their thoughts about the Wall and its place in their lives and in the life of America. As the week progressed, I learned more about the war and its lasting effects. I took pictures for people who posed against the Wall for posterity. I witnessed reunions between vets who hadn't seen each other for decades. I shared my Kleenex. I watched as person after person placed a hand on the Wall, and I realized that it is with our senses that we come to understand the memorial and its role in the life of America.

By speaking with people about their experiences, I realized that I did have memories of Vietnam. I remembered a friend's brother who came home from the war, but never talked about what happened. I thought about the Saturdays when we weren't allowed to go into town because the college kids were protesting. And then there was the time when my uncle's girlfriend and I baked cookies, which we carefully decorated and packed into boxes to send to her brother, who was in a place called Vietnam. Plattsburgh was the site of a SAC base and during my junior high years I had friends whose dads worked there. A lot of kids came and went as their fathers were transferred about. I remember one friend in particular, who came in seventh grade. Charlotte was from Texas and was only around

for a year. I always thought it was strange that she had two last names, but I never felt it was my place to ask why. I suspect now that her father had been killed in Vietnam and her mother had remarried another pilot, who was soon after transferred and immediately sent overseas. I lost touch with her. I only hope that she didn't lose a second father to Vietnam. Charlie, if you ever read this, my mom still uses that recipe for michigans that you figured out by taste–testing, and I'm sorry I didn't know then to ask the right questions to understand your life. The Wall has helped provide those questions.

The Vietnam Veterans Memorial is almost austere in its simplicity. Two polished walls stretch toward the Washington Monument on the east and the Lincoln Memorial on the west, linking America's past with the present. Unlike the other memorials, you can't see the Wall from a car. You have to approach it. Enter its domain. At its outer edges, the Wall is less than a foot high, hardly appropriate for a national monument. Yet at the apex where the two walls meet, the memorial rises toward the sky, engulfing us with its height. At its center the Wall begins to make sense. The names, which began on a single line, have multiplied to the point where they surround us. All of a sudden the implication is clear: the Wall represents what might have been.

Looking at the Wall, we see the world reflected: sun, moon, clouds, the trees in the distance, the people standing next to us. Finally, we see ourselves on its surface. These reflections remind us that the Wall is as much about the present as the past. We see our world mirrored in the names we find there and realize that the slightest movement changes the view. No image is permanent on the Wall. Only the names are eternal.

Most of us touch the Wall. Our touch is tentative at first, but grows more assured as we discover its warmth. The black granite captures the sun, giving it back to our fingertips as they trace the names carved on its face. The list is chronological, beginning in July 1959 and ending in May 1975. Everyone is equal on the Wall; there is no rank, only the order of casualty. Each name has a diamond or a plus next to it. Diamonds confirm death, a plus means unanswered questions for families who still wait.

The Wall is a quiet place. There might be two people or twenty thousand present, but the sounds are still the same: hushed whispers, reverential comments, or just silence. Being at the Wall is a holy experience. It is Mecca for the Vietnam generation—America's Wailing Wall. It is the place where we come to mourn, to grieve, to reflect as a nation on the true cost of war. Personal opinion about the legitimacy of the war is irrelevant at the Wall. The only thing that matters is the recognition of life interrupted, the loss of potential, the families and friends who go on alone, comforted only by memory. It doesn't matter that we didn't know any of them personally. The act of coming to the Wall unites us with the people who did and from them we glimpse meaning.

I spent hours at the Wall during that week in 1993. I'd go in the morning right after dawn to watch the sun rise through the autumn mist. I'd stay until late at night after the tourists had gone home. I was at the Wall at mid-day, when bus loads would arrive on their choreographed tours of the city, when office workers strolled by on their lunch hours, when joggers cut through on their way to the reflecting pool. I saw the Wall in light and in darkness. With crowds and with solitary veterans. It is where I now go during every visit to Washington. The Wall is no longer a foreign place.

For many the Wall is a place where they come to say good-bye and lay the past to rest. For others, the Wall is a beginning, the start of a journey as they seek to understand. For the Vietnam veterans, their families and friends, it is a place where finally they are "welcomed home." It is a place of reconciliation and healing.

Upon completion of the Wall, many people thought the job was done. But it was really only the beginning. The memorial not only honors the dead and missing, but offers the hope of healing to those left behind.

Over forty million people are closely related to the names on the Wall. Many of them are still paying the price of the war. Many have wounds still waiting to be healed. The Friends of the Vietnam Veterans Memorial[2] grew out of the need to help these people. This national not-for-profit, nonpolitical service organization offers several free programs to bring the healing effects of the Wall to thousands of families, friends, and veterans who were touched by the Vietnam War.

Larry Powell's photographs capture the essence of the Vietnam Veterans Memorial—the feeling of reconciliation that shaped its design and the healing that takes place there. Throughout these pages, you will meet the people who come to the Wall. The power and simplicity of the photos are overwhelming. *Hunger of the Heart* is Larry Powell's personal journey, his visual memories of the Vietnam Veterans Memorial.

Cara Sutherland

---

1. National Park Service, Museum and Curatorial Services, 1100 Ohio Dr., S. W., Room 134, Washington, DC 20242.
2. Friends of the Vietnam Veterans Memorial, 2030 Clardendon Blvd., Suite 412, Arlington, VA 22201.

AT THE WALL

Over one million people travel to the Vietnam Veterans Memorial every year. Visitors are found at the Wall twenty-four hours a day. For many, it is a visit of great sacrifice, both financially and emotionally. Visiting the Wall is an individual experience. For some, it is best done alone without an audience of family and friends. Others need the love and support of families and friends to get through it.

For some veterans moving close to the Wall, actually touching the Wall, is too much of a risk. These veterans are known as the "tree-line vets." It may take them several visits before they actually can reach the Wall.

A dedicated group of volunteers help the National Park Service staff the monument. Many of these volunteers are veterans or mothers, sisters, brothers, children, and friends of those who are named on the Wall. They come at their own expense and are often using vacation time from their jobs. Recognized by the yellow baseball caps they wear, these volunteers are a wealth of knowledge and information, which they share with those who visit. They help visitors find the names they are looking for, offering comfort and support to the many who come to find healing and peace.

I will never forget you! You will always be a part of me— part of you lives in me. I will carry your memory forever and I will make people confront that memory—the memory of what was done to us. If I could, I would lead each person in hand past this monument and make them read each name and imagine each life that was cut short. I promise you, my friends, I will never let them forget the price you paid.

I tried so much to keep you alive the day you died and I tried to keep your spirit alive while the country for which you died tried to forget you. At last you live again but not just in the hearts of us who loved you. You live in America's heart as well.

Well, Mom's been meaning to see you, but the work's just never done, and Dad just seems to sit around and stare. Well, I just know they're really proud of you. You served your country like you had to do. It'll take a little time, but they'll be there. I guess I miss you most of all. You were more than a brother, you were my friend. I thought we'd be together, but so suddenly it had to end. I never thought I'd never see you again. I would have stood out by the airport, waiting for your flight to be called. I didn't think we'd see your name up on that wall.

I share this with those of you who come to this hallowed wall of names—remembering, seeking comfort and solace for the losses we all suffered as a result of Vietnam. Know that others share your sorrow and pray for you and those you knew and love who are named here forever on this starkly beautiful memorial.

James,

Sorry they wouldn't keep it down longer so I could get you brother. I wish it was me instead of you. Just wanted you to know I love you brother. Still talk to Cathy, and your babies. They're grown and proud of you. You're me, and I'm you. I'll always watch over them for you brother. God bless I'll see ya soon James. Just thought I would let you know everthing's OK.
The Doc

Do you remember when you didn't need to use stamps? I can write free now too. Never thought this would be your new address: Panel 22 West, Line 27.

I passed the Wall yesterday and started sobbing. I couldn't come any closer. Today I'm back to find your name, make a rubbing, to make my amends to you and to grieve.
. . . I hope seeing your name and leaving this letter will help me heal the conflict inside.

Your name is on a black wall in D.C., but I'm sorry to say that it's a little below ground—kind of like how Charlie was! You look over a nice green—a place like we used to play football on back home. A lot of people walk by all day—you can tell the Vets—we are the ones who don't have to ask about the size or type of material used to make the wall. We just stand and look, not caring who sees us cry—just like no one cared who died.

COMING HOME

The Vietnam Veterans Memorial was created as a result of the efforts of Veterans. They raised the money, lobbied Congress, found a de-sign-er, and built the Wall. For many of these men and women, the Memorial represents their true coming home. It is the place where they finally receive a long overdue welcome.

Many items left by veterans are memories of the in-country experience, a part of daily life in Vietnam. Small offerings found at the Wall— a can of beer, a package of cigarettes, a dollar bill—represent communication between the living and the dead, the idea of a debt ultimately repaid.

Perhaps relinquishing these reminders of war is a means of release or maybe a gesture of appreciation for a fallen comrade. According to one veteran, leaving something at the Wall was a way to connect with his friends whose names he found there.

We crept "point" together and pulled "drag" together. We lay crouched in cold mud and were drenched by monsoons. We sweated buckets and endured the heat of dry season. We burnt at least a thousand leeches off one another and went through a gallon of insect repellent a day that the bugs were irresistibly attracted to. . . . You got a bronze star, a silver star, survived 18 months of one demon hell after another, only to walk into a booby trapped bunker and all of a sudden you had no face or chest. I never cried. My chest becomes unbearably painful and my throat tightens so I can't even croak, but I haven't cried. I wanted to, just couldn't. I think I can today. Damm, I'm crying now.

How angry I was to find you here—though I knew that you would be. I've wished so hard that I could have saved you. I would give my life if somehow it would bring you all back.

This world has changed. I am sorry you don't share it with me. I am sorry your name is here. I ask why mine is not.

We grew up together. We served together. You died and I lived. I never could understand that. You were a much better person than me. I'll always remember you. Life has never been the same without you.

It has been a long time. But I will never forget you—or Nam—but I have finally come <u>home</u> today.

November 9, 1993

Richard Lakin:

Well old friend, this is the first time I've had the guts to come and pay my respects. It's been more than twenty years. But not a day has gone by that I haven't thought about you and some of the talks we had. I wonder why you're there and I'm here and if somehow you wouldn't have done more with your life than I've done with mine. I never did call your family when I came home. Went to Canada for about 15 years. Then it all seemed like so long in the past, I just didn't want to open any of their wounds. I wish I could have traded places with you. I know your death has affected many more persons than even I can imagine. The impact on me and those who loved and respected you will be there for the rest of our lives. You may be gone but you will be in our hearts as long as we draw breath. I can even hear your voice sometimes. When I do, I try to jot what I hear. Please keep it up.
 Be at peace if you can, for many of those still alive find it impossible and little understanding of our situation. But soon we will all be reunited and I guess that is as it should be. Makes you wonder what this is all about don't it? That's it for this visit. Doubt I 'll come here again. Too many memories and too much pain. But we'll talk again. Of that, I am sure.

Scanlen

Our skin was not the same but our hearts were. I've missed you soul brother. Travel in peace. You are in good company with our brothers. This ten pack is on me. I've come to have one last smooth one with you.

This is a tribute to all of you who died so valiantly, in a war that was not your own; yet you died anyway. I leave this patch as a gift from all of us who were there with you but are yet alive today, to thank you for your sacrifice.

I'm standing at the Vietnam Memorial today as I've done several times before; the same feeling comes over me—that day in March 1966 was a tough one. I don't know how I survived—by all rights, my wounds should have killed me too. It wasn't easy seeing you laying in that rice paddy. It took me five years to see your folks, but I was glad that I did. I don't know if I'll ever be back here again. In case I don't, let me say, "So Long Buddy."

To watch you die has been the most painful encounter of my life. I prayed for you, my brother of war. When I turned my head in hopelessness your breath of life stopped. I could no longer hear your breathing then. I knew that you were at peace. Bless you, for you are the hero.

Twenty-five years ago I departed from Travis Air Force Base and arrived in Saigon on this date above [March 6, 1969]. I had many FRIENDS that were killed in country and I am dedicating my field equipment to those who never arrived home alive. I only hope that someone will place my field gear where future generations will see what we had to sacrifice for this country! <u>*This is my last Patrol!!*</u>

The peace of the memorial belies the terrible hell of mud and fire where you fell, and since that day a whole generation has grown to maturity. Even so, friend, rest assured the flag yet flies at home, on summer nights taps still echo from Harrison's woods, lakes and hills, and on deep cold winter nights, the lake ice sings still.

I think about you guys frequently but mostly about the others without names that we killed. I don't know why. The wall is nice. You all seem to be at rest here.

19

I lay this rose

In the tradition of

And in the MEMORY of

LEWIS B. PULLER, JR.

May he now be resting in PEACE with his troops

Top made it out of Nam, but it killed him anyway, in 1973. Arty, too. He killed himself in 1969, eight months after you were lost. I thought about it a long time, but things happened that kept me from it, just like that first night of Tet in '68. I wondered then, and still wonder now, why it was you and not me.

I have long admired you and still miss you. I never could walk in your moccasins at 1/7. Thanks for visiting me before you died. I still remember the watch. Pray for me. P.S. We always knew that one day you would win the CMH.

SYMBOLS OF HONOR

Leaving medals at the Vietnam Veterans Memorial can be viewed as a rejection of the military experience, a way for the owner to move beyond the past and live in the present and for the future. It may be a statement of anger and frustration as in the case of a veteran who left his Congressional Medal of Honor as a result of his disillusionment over American foreign policy.

On the other hand, the donor may be choosing to honor his or her fallen comrades by leaving something of great personal importance. Medals and awards are highly prized, indicative of courage and achievement by their recipients. Accompanying notes are often poignant and go into great detail on acts of bravery accomplished by someone whose name is on the Wall. Wrote one donor:

"Here are the Battle Ribbons awarded to you for giving your life at Con Thien South Viet-Nam Sept 7, 67. You will never see them. You will never wear them. But you deserve them. I thought you should have them."

Attached to this letter are my service medals. I don't need them to show that I was there. I have your faces to remind me in my sleep. I will leave now to return to my safe place. Rest well, my brothers, may the wind be to your backs and the sun in your faces. On the day we meet again, please do one thing, "Tell me your name."

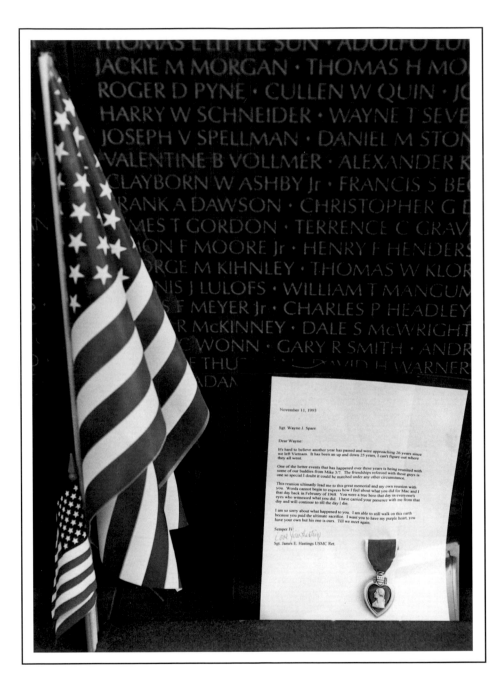

I never met you, Grandpa, but I love you and am
proud of you! I am looking forward to the day
when we meet in Heaven!
Your Grandson,
Pete

RANDALL E COLE · RONNIE C CURETON ·
IAN J FRANKS · EULAS F GREGORY · MICHA
ROBERT A KANESKI · CLARENCE DAWKINS

For Our Son
WITH · LOVE

For those who served,
sacrificed, and died in
Vietnam and those who
died at home after the
war. Peace at last.

Dear Leon and Kenny,

Here's a flag for you guys that you weren't able to fly I'll always fly one for you guys & for all the ideals for which you made the ultimate sacrifice. I should have been there with you, but the Lord destined my journey otherwise. I'll see you Marines in heaven, cause we spent our time in Hell. I love you guys.

Mike

LIFE INTERRUPTED

Each of the 58,196 names on the Vietnam Veterans Memorial equals a life interrupted. For the people left behind, the Wall is public acknowledgement of their grief and loss.

Coming to the Memorial is a ritual for many people. It is a place where they can reconnect with their loved ones and share their strength with first-time visitors.

Although Veterans Day and Memorial Day are periods of high visitation, other holidays such as Christmas, Easter, and Father's Day find families gathering together at the Wall. As the years go by, the Wall is where generations meet. Mothers put children to rest, their boys and girls who will never grow old. Children talk to their fathers saying, "They tell me I look a lot like you." Brothers and sisters relay family news. Parents introduce their children to grandparents they'll never know.

I came to visit you today. I haven't ever felt so close to you before. I never got a chance to know you but I love you very much. There isn't a day goes by that Mom doesn't think of you. . . . You're gone from us now but we'll all be together again one day. You'll never be forgotten, you still live in everyone of us. I'm really proud to be your son. I hope I can be as good a man as you were.

Even though I never really knew you, you have still meant the world to me. Thank you daddy, for giving me 3 years of your life. Remembering you through photos, I can only say I love you Daddy. Happy Father's Day. A part of me died with you. Love—
Your Son Joe

Before he left, he taught me how to drive his car. Then he left it to me to take care of it "til he got back."
"Dad survived Iwo Jima, Guadalcanal and all that. I'm a Marine. I'll be back. Take care of my car." I've still got the car. I would rather have my big brother back.

Brother

I never really got to say "I Love You"
I didn't know what death really was...
Growing up without you was like a piece
of my heart was gone.... But coming here to
the **WALL** is like a dream that come true.
Being able to let go of my hatred towards
the Wasicu for taking you from me. It was
hard, but seeing all the Vet's, made me
realize that you went to defend Unci —
Maka for the Lakota Oyate and all the
Nations. I come to let you know and to let
you go, so you may be with your relatives
over that Beautiful River.. to yet!!
Another and better Life, where you are
Welcomed with open Arms and Love.

"I LOVE You
Brother"

Your Sister

"June Bug"

I miss you and think of you so much. . . . I'm bringing "Teddy Bear" and a picture of your loved race car. I realize that they can't stay there long, but they are yours and I want them to be with you. In time, I hope we can all be together.

Hi Dad. The last time you saw me I was just starting to walk. I really didn't get to know you or you to know me. Well, here it is 22 years later and I am married to a wonderful girl. Her name is Sue. We have been married three years and next year when we come back to the Wall like we do every year, I will be showing your name to your grandchild and will say that this is your grandfather's name. He or she will know that for some reason you were a great man. I knew little about you until one night I asked Mom about you and talked to some of your old friends to find out who you really were. All the people I have talked to said that you would have done just about anything for anybody. I think you and me are alot alike. I became a volunteer fireman to help people anyway I can. I miss you and wish you were here today so I didn't have to come to this Black Wall. But you thought it was the right thing to do by going to Vietnam.

Waddaya say, kid—I brought you flowers. I always brought you flowers, didn't I? Picked from the neighbors yards on the way to the school bus. . . . It's how we fell in love. And then I gave you daisies in the midst of all those white slabs of death.

PERSONAL MOMENTS

The Vietnam Veterans Memorial serves as a witness to personal moments between the living and the dead. Offerings left at the Wall mark time, representing the healing process that the Memorial inspires. Although the item is left behind, the feelings that inspired the offering remain in the heart of the donor.

At first, only those people with personal ties left things at the Wall. Veterans spoke to veterans. Families mourned loved ones. Friends reminisced with their buddies. The first items collected represent these personal connections, gestures between the past and the present.

The collection evolves as the Wall matures. No longer just a repository of individual memory, the Wall is now a gathering place for all Americans. As with the friends and families, these visitors also feel compelled to add their thoughts and gifts to the Wall. Children frequently write to unknown names, thanking them for their service to the country. There is a sense of the wider human community in these items.

I come to this place with heavy heart. I feel the guilt of this nation. You who asked for so little, and gave so much. When so many of us ask for so much, and have given so little to this great country.   A Citizen

Do you remember that water buffalo Dad gave you when he came back from Clark AB in 1965? Well, you gave it to me to keep when you went into the Army in 1966 and I've had it ever since. I figure it's time to give it back to you now. That buffalo has been with me through 18 moves and I saved it from the packers this week for you. I want it to be remembered that you were a real person who lived and was loved very much.

As I prepare to go to Washington, I know it's you I wish to see, but I'll see your name darling. It means you are not coming home to me.

To all Vietnam Veterans: We are thankful to those who gave their best, under the worst of circumstances. Like many others, we still seek to understand war. We love and appreciate our freedom. God bless America.

Dear Soldier

How do I begin to put into words my feelings as I stand here before this tribute to you?

I was one of the thousands who believed that the war was wrong. I protested—but please know that I protested against the war, not you. I wanted you home on the college campus or with your family and friends—working, playing, crying, laughing HERE at home . . . not THERE dying.

Many times when asked why I never married I would say jokingly that the one with my name on him was probably in some rice field in Nam, never to return. But it's not a joke.

We are all diminished because you are gone. However we are all also enhanced because you so bravely gave of yourself for our precious beliefs of liberty and justice.

Thank you, soldier. You are in my heart and my prayers. You are my hero.

Please don't ask me why it took so long to get here. My life and feelings have been out of control for all of these years. Hopefully, this visit and God will guide me in the right direction and take this pain from my heart and mind, and allow you to rest in peace.

According to Park Rangers, this bear was left "naked" at The Wall. Throughout the day, other visitors "dressed him" and added to his gear.

Well here you are, making another lasting impression on me and everyone else who sees you! I love you so much. I have dreamed of the day you'll come home and finally be my Dad. . . . I'm 23 now! I sure look a lot different from six years old. You'd be very proud of me. They say I'm a lot like you. I can see it, too! I have never forgotten you. I knew that you were Santa Claus, but I didn't want to spoil it for you.

GROUP MEMORIALS

Although visiting the Vietnam Veterans Memorial is a highly personal experience, it is also the scene of group interaction. Throughout the year, rituals and ceremonies are enacted at the Wall in memory of fallen comrades and missing friends. These events are public in nature, but reflect the individual experience of their participants.

Local groups come to celebrate their home town heroes. Veterans honor the missing. Unit survivors remember the lost. Each occurrence reinforces the sense of memory and history taking place at the Wall, finding expression in numerous wreaths and ceremonial objects left there.

The military tradition of taking care of your own is played out at the Memorial. Groups who come to the Wall offer financial and emotional support to their members who might not be able to come there on their own. Veterans comfort each other and offer a shoulder to lean on when words aren't nearly enough. Facing the Wall means coming to terms with the past in order to go on into the future.

I was your leader and I have not forgotten you. Nor have I forgotten how you each gave your lives to rescue wounded comrades from a nameless hill in a worthless country. I am sorry I never wrote your families back then, but I was wounded myself a few days later. I have finally begun to write my, and our, story after eighteen years. I haven't gotten to March 1, 1968, yet. I had to come down last night and tell you about it before I wrote about it. I also wanted to spend a little time with you on the night before you die again. I wanted to be with you again when the clock struck midnight and your numbers came up.

In 1968 we spent some time together. We tried not to get close for reasons only you and I can understand, however we did. We laughed, drank beer, played cards, and even cried together. Our camp was open to you and yours to us. . . . At approx. 10:30 A.M. I watched tracer rounds from a 50 cal. firing upon a spotter plane. I knew no small group of VCs would fire or carry the 50 cal. It wasn't a hit and run outfit. I radioed in at about 10:45. By 11:00 A.M. the decision was made that you would go for the kill. As I helped and watched you ready for your mission, I recall saying "I'll see you ugly mugs for lunch." I had no idea you would never eat again.

Yourself reflected,
Reflective,
Unable to walk past all those,
Names,
And Mementoes
Without thought,
For finally, there has been,
Both burial, And reminder.
A giant sunken headstone
At which to lay
Flowers, flags, newspaper clippings
Hats, sea–rations, and memories.

When I'm happy, I think you share it
and when I'm down I think you guys
would be pissed. You know I loved you
guys and I miss you terribly. We were
tight. I wish it all turned out better.
Can't think of you guys as angels. More
like Valhalla, drinking beer, pissing
foam, counting the days 'til we go home.
Sometimes I sit in the dark and smoke—
I see you in the smoke not like ghosts,
but sitting calm—waiting to move out.

*The day you did come home
is etched forever in my soul.
When I visit you here at the
"Wall," the overwhelming
sense of your presence brings
a flood of memories and tears
from deep inside.*

Semper Fi

<u>*Sept 9*</u> *India and Kolo got hit real hard while they were patrolling the area. The last report here was last night and the fighting was still going on. The kick in the ass is that 30—40 of the men were "short-timers" in the company and had only 10 days left before they would be taken out of the field. Now they are wounded, killed, or missing. . . .*

<u>*Sept 11*</u> *Today they pulled them out of the field. There is not much left of 3rd Bn., 26th Reg. India Company. They went to Con Thien with 168 combat marines. It now has 72 men left. . . .*

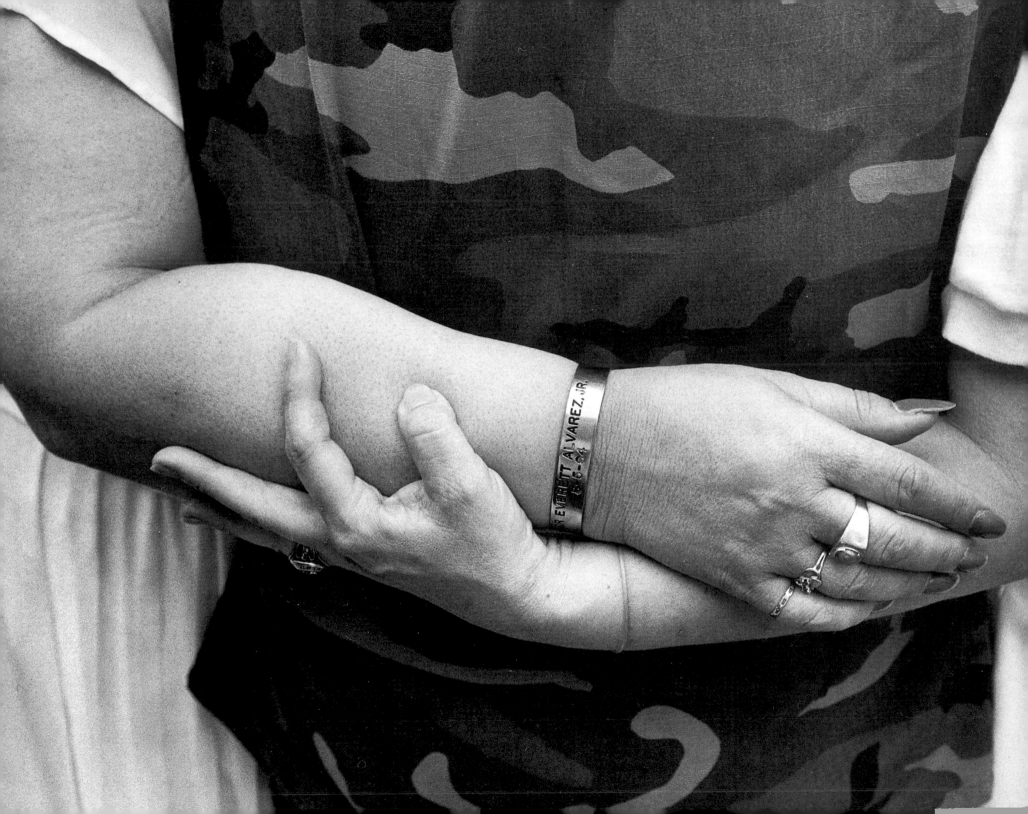

MISSING AND UNACCOUNTED

"You are not forgotten." This quiet sentence is the core of the POW/MIA movement.

Items left at the Wall often reflect the passion of the POW/MIA movement—both past and present. During the Vietnam War, the wearing of a POW/MIA bracelet was an expression of solidarity and compassion for the families of the missing men. This practice is carried on today and offers comfort to those left behind.

The names of the many soldiers who were unaccounted for at the end of the war are marked with a + on the Vietnam Veterans Memorial. In the event that they are confirmed dead, the mark is changed to a diamond. Should they return, the + will be encircled. At present, nearly 1300 names on the Wall remain marked with a +. Their families and friends still wait.

Some consider the Wall a national tombstone where the families and friends of the missing and unaccounted for can mourn. The Memorial fills a need for those who lack an individual cemetery plot to visit.

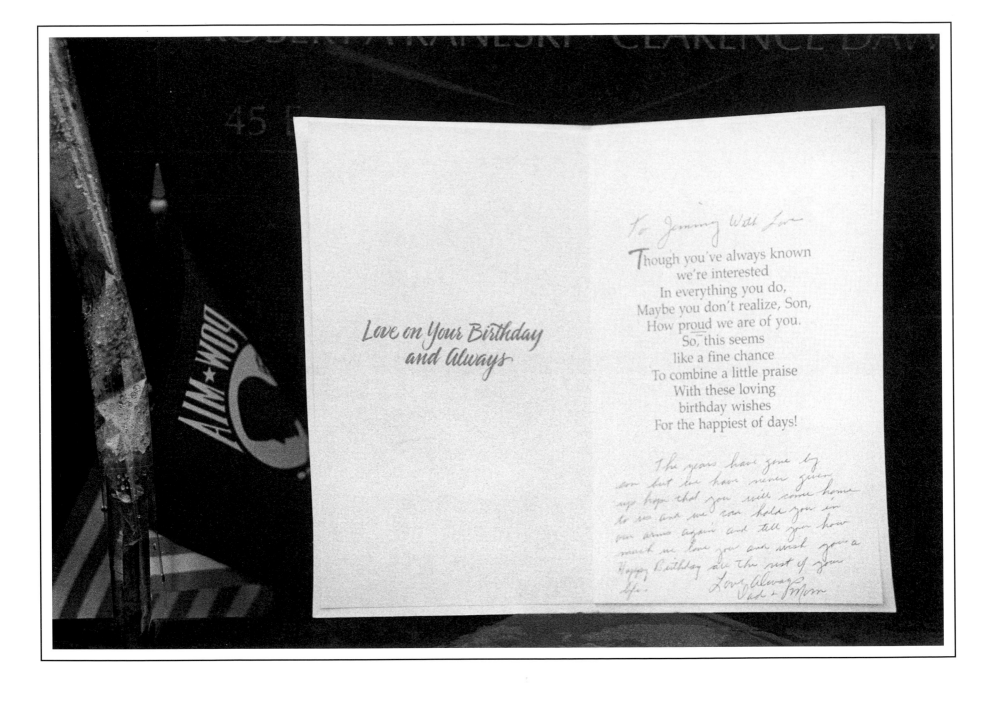

Love on Your Birthday
and Always

To Jimmy With Love

Though you've always known
we're interested
In everything you do,
Maybe you don't realize, Son,
How proud we are of you.
So, this seems
like a fine chance
To combine a little praise
With these loving
birthday wishes
For the happiest of days!

The years have gone by
son but we have never given
up hope that you will come home
to us and we can hold you in
our arms again and tell you how
much we love you and wish you a
Happy Birthday all the rest of your
life.
Love Always,
Dad + Mom

Came by again to see your name, funny that's all I have. Today's my birthday. I really do miss you and wish you'll come home soon. Maybe they will release you tomorrow.

Dear Daddy, Sorry this is on a bubblegum wrapper but I didn't know that I would be stopping by today. You know I can't resist. I wish you could have been here for graduation. I graduated 4th.

The pathway and the ground at this memorial have been deep-watered by the tears of thousands of Americans who remember and who care. I hope that someday soon our tears of sadness will turn to tears of joy and thanksgiving when some of the crosses of the MIAs are changed to stars. God bless you all, especially those who served in Vietnam.

To all the "Grunts" missing and others who gave their lives for an ungrateful nation. You will always live in my heart. A grateful Florida Vietnam Veteran.

AFTER THE WAR

Long after the Vietnam War formally ended, the war continues in the hearts and minds of many veterans and their families. More Vietnam veterans have died here at home as a direct result of the war than were killed in action. For many, after returning home, communication was difficult, misunderstandings multiplied, and families broke apart without even knowing what went wrong. Illness, alcoholism, hopelessness, and homelessness are only a few of the problems that have taken a toll on those trying to come to terms with the horrors of war. Many of the items left at the Wall reflect these problems, especially that of Agent Orange. These issues are a continual reminder of the long-term consequences of war.

In recent years, current affairs and political debate have found expression at the Wall. The Wall has become a place for both protest and support of many issues. It is a witness to the forces that continue to shape this country.

If I could,

*   I would heal you from the memory that fails with the shed of every tear,*

*   I would heal you from the suffering, that you've endured from year to year,*

*   I would heal the pain of all your families, this war managed to destroy,*

*   And I would give back to every mother, the happy face of her "little boy."*

If I could . . . I would.

You gave your life for all of us, man. I wouldn't leave you there alone. You are me and I am you. I will always remain "on guard duty." You and I know why I can't let go.

In Vietnam, at age 20, I was put in charge of a river boat. Now every time I get on a boat I only see the red blood running over the deck and into the water. I try to take my 2 sons fishing but we never stay out long. The fish don't seem to bite when I take them out, like they do when they go with someone else's father. They are too young to understand that their father does not like the reflections he sees in the water.

83

Perhaps, now I can bury you; at least in my soul. Perhaps, now, I won't see you again night after night when the war re-appears and we are once more amidst the myriad hells that Vietnam engulfed us in.

Dear Vets,

We never knew any of you, but we've heard of your courage in history class. We were touched when
we heard how badly you were treated after fighting your hardest. Many people now come to this
Memorial to honor your bravery. We are two of millions.

You are truely remembered.

DAUGHTERS OF WAR

Only in recent years has America begun to learn about the service of her daughters—the invisible veterans of Vietnam. During the Vietnam conflict, over 265,000 women served in America's armed forces. Few Americans realized what these veterans suffered. Their stress equaled that of the soldier.

Unlike the men, American military women in Vietnam were all volunteers. An estimated 11,000 were stationed in-country. Eight of their names are recorded on the Wall. Thousands more American women participated in the Red Cross and other service organizations. More than fifty of them gave their lives in Vietnam, but because they were civilians, their names do not appear on the Wall.

Veterans Day 1993 marked the unveiling of the Women's Statue. The unveiling and dedication of this statue represents the completion of the Vietnam Veterans Memorial.

. . . and so I go on seeing the wounded when I hear a chopper,
washing your blood from my hands,
hearing your screams in my sleep,
scrubbing the smell of your burned bodies from my clothes,
feeling your pain, which never eases,
fighting a war that never ends.

We did what we could but it was not enough, because I found you
here. All of you are not just names on this wall; you are alive. Your
blood's on my hands, your screams in my ears, your eyes in my soul. I
told you you'd be alright but I lied. Please forgive me. You told me
about your wife, your kids, your girl, your mother. Then you died. I
should have done more. Your pain is ours. Please, God. I'll never forget
your faces. I can't, you're still alive.

I don't remember the names, only the young faces. I feel guilt for failing so often, but finally I feel pride that I tried. What does anyone know at 19? I've wanted to come for years. I wasn't ready, too many mixed emotions. I love you all. I'll never forget you. Never.

Love, not Anger

Understanding, not Frustration

Patience, not Impatience

Truth not Lies

The love of a daughter is like the light of the Sun—If a father

listens and is lucky, very lucky—He will walk in the sunshine too—

For a very very long time.

I love you—

A Vet & a Very Proud Father, Thank you Shannon, you were RIGHT.

I leave with you symbols of the war you lost your life in. I am a nurse, like you and a former member of the 312 Evac Hospital Unit. I now work for peace so that young women & men will never have to lose their lives again. May God rest your Soul.

To all my sisters who served when their country called, with a courage and perseverance recognized by few, I present this painting, with great admiration and respect for the painful job you did, and I bear part of the shame for the respect you did not receive, an extreme injustice. . . . Until we meet again with all our brothers and sisters whom we will never forget, I salute you all from my heart.

*I went to Vietnam to heal and came home silently wounded.
I went to Vietnam to heal and still awaken from nightmares
about those we couldn't save. I went to Vietnam to heal and
came home to grieve for those we sent home blind,
paralyzed, limbless, mindless. I went to Vietnam to heal and
discovered I am not God.*

Is war over simply because it ends?